Mother Earth

trumps

man

is a collection of poems that tell the story of a man's
life-long-love-affair with Mother Earth...

by

Charles Portolano

3/18/17

Mother Earth trumps man

by Charles Portolano

Copyrighted 2017 by Charles Portolano

ISBN: 978-0-578-19047-1

First Edition - 250 press run

This book of poetry is dedicated to

Mother Earth, Vivi and Valerie, long may they live...

Other books of poetry by Charles Portolano:

Inspired by Their Spirits - Wyndham Hall Press
The Nature of Darkness - Wyndham Hall Press
The Soul Decision - Wyndham Hall Press
Firsts (written with Valerie Portolano) * chapbook - RWG Press
All Eyes on US - RWG Press
Storytelling - Port Publications
The little, lingering, white lies we allow ourselves to live with – As Is Arts Press

For addition copies, please make out a check to The Avocet for $12.00 for each copy and send to:

The Avocet
P.O. Box 19186
Fountain Hills, AZ 85269

or contact us at cportolano@hotmail.com

The Avocet Publishing Press – 2017

A call of the wild

Bundled up to brave
the air so cruel and crisp
it freezes the lining
of one's nostrils
if not covered up.
The full moon glows
in the cloudy night sky,
making long, scary shadows
reaching out over the frozen
clearing of the bare, bony
birch trees standing before us.
My younger brother and I
crunch the hard snow
following the wolf's call,
caroming through the valley,
bouncing off the mountains,
calling from the darkness.
'For what? For whom?'
Standing as sentries,
guarding some secret,
these birch trees spook
us as we hurry past them
to the ridge edge to witness
the black silhouette
of a lone wolf
on a stony, protruding crag,
arching its head back
to howl its heart out
throughout the valley.
We stand so still, the hair
on our necks rising, as we
take in this sight, waiting
until another wolf
calls from far off
in the vast, empty space
of the utter darkness
between the two mountains;
filling us with a wildness…

A deer gift given

Stepping on twisted twigs
alerts the nibbling deer
and her two dear does
that we are near,
we both fear
they will dart away,
as my younger brother
has a shamefaced grimace
and a tear in his eye,
knowing he has spoiled
our chances of getting
within inches of them,
to quietly watch
them eat in peace,
but the deer and her does
stand frozen in their spot
as we stop in our place,
not breathing,
not twitching a muscle,
just taking in
the gift of this moment
so rarely given.
The deer turns her head
to gaze upon us,
sensing we are harmless
she graces us
by rubbing her cheek
against the tiny face
of the smaller doe
as if to let her know
she has nothing to fear
from the two of us
standing so near;
we watch in disbelief
as they eat the green bush
until they are finished,
then quietly disappear
into the dense forest.

Time among Trees

Trees are Cathedrals,
sanctuaries,
casting long shadows,
while not uttering
a word to be heard,
but do they speak,
they do listen
when spoken to,
they do not preach,
but reach out,
teaching me to take
only what I need,
never to want more;
as I walk among them,
the wind whispers
the secrets the trees
wish to share with me:
to be cool, calm, and
always collected
makes the air easier
for all to breathe.
It is there that I learn
to pray under them
for forgiveness,
for the damage we've done;
told to give life back
to Mother Earth
by digging a hole
to plant a tree
so its roots grow
strong in the sweet soil
of Mother's soul;
told to help create a forest
for others, so they too
can walk among trees
for trees teach patience,
they teach peace;
they know not of war
as they inch their way
high into the heavens.

Skating away this Winter day

Early we race along the frozen river,
where Spring through Fall, we go fishing;
now our breaths before us,
like trains blowing smoke,
billowing up and out,
warning all we are coming around the bend,
coming full-steam,
streaming down, making our way
along the meandering course
that this river takes,
following the winding way downstream
twisting
        and
turning,
      then returning
on itself;
with wonderful,
           white,
              rolling
                  hills
on both sides,
their bare trees whispering for Spring, as
are the meadows filled with powdery snow.
The wind smacks against our exposed cheeks,
our sunglasses on for the glare off the snow,
we race each other through the cold air,
feeling like we had taken flight, soaring,
racing to the far corners of our little town.

Catching our breaths, we rest under the oaks;
with little wind, we can hear the trees
sigh, just waiting, so still, for Spring
to finally come, but today we skate
along this winding, old-friend-of-a-river,
frozen for us to frolic upon until nightfall.

Starting over

The dead tree is still
standing, but their nest
of three years has been
blown away due to storms.
Not waiting for his mate
to return from Mexico,
he begins bringing branches
to rebuild their old home,
using his beak to force each
branch into its place, to stand
the test of rain and wind.
He sees her on the horizon,
he flies out to meet her,
to greet her, with swoops
and circles they fly doing
the sky dance, aerial acrobatics
of their love for one another.
Their high-pitched squeals
of joy can be heard around
the cove after a long Winter
apart from each other.
He soars high in the sky
to dive straight into the bay
with his razor sharp talons
hooking a large bass
to present to her as a token
of his love of her.
Soon she is off collecting
eelgrass to add to the inside
of the growing nest.
She covers over the branches,
making a deep depression
in the middle for her eggs
to rest during incubation.
He makes trip after trip,
gathering up sticks of wood,
building a home for their
soon to be brood of three.

The Bald Eagle

The bold, bald eagle
scours the sky,
eyeing the earth
and beyond
from atop
its mountain perch
searching for food
for its three eaglets
in the valley below.

Suddenly springing
onto the sunlit thermals
with wings spread wide
rising on the warm air,
up-drifting along
the mountain slopes,
gliding in flight,
soaring in solitude,
seeing everything.

Sighting some
slight movement
in the bushes below,
with one swift swoop
of those wondrous wings,
she dives down,
descending upon her prey,
talons poised
for an instant kill.

A sudden, single gunshot
shatters the silence.
Forever changed witnessing
this from that far ridge.

Coyote

In the light of day
coming out
of the wash,
a young male
crosses the road
with a slight limp,
right in front
of my car
forcing me
to a full stop,
staring me down
with such distrust
almost contempt
for he knows
of our desire
to destroy him,
but by adapting
he out-smarted us,
now flourishing
among us,
he turns his back
to me, crossing
the asphalt road,
his bushy tail
shoots straight up,
stiff as only
a true dissident
would dare do,
and with a wave
of his bushy tail
he disappears
into the wash
on the other side
of the road;
I had to laugh.

Living in the moment

The pine scent saturates
my searching consciousness
as I come upon fresh tracks
of a coyote and a cottontail
in the light dusting on this
early morning, December day.
Down-wind of them,
I follow through the forest
between the thick trees until
I see the crouching coyote
ready to pounce upon
the rabbit hidden in the bush.
The crackle of crushing twigs
startles the coyote;
he stares straight at me
in indignant disbelief.
The whitetail bolts away
with a zig, then a
          sharp zag, gone
with the crazed coyote
biting at her bushy tail,
just inches within
his snapping jaws,
with me in full pursuit.
My heart racing as
they fly full speed
over the edge of the ridge.
The coyote loses its footing,
tumbles, then slides
down the slippery slope.
I skid to a full stop
watching the sure-footed
rabbit run away.
The scowl on the coyote
told the whole story for
I could still taste near-death
stir on the slight wind
whispering through the trees.

Whistling Straits

is where we would go
to be alone.
She knew how to wiggle
and wind her way
down deep
into the canyon, where
few have gone before,
down to the river
where the wind
runs wild with
the rushing water.
Singing sweetly
like the sirens, they
call her into
the middle of the river,
knee high she would go
and just let that
wind sing sweetly
through the straits,
rushing by her,
rushing through
her open fingers,
brushing back her hair;
the air so strong
she claimed she could
feel it stretch
the skin taut of her face,
peel off some of her sins.
Oh, how she loved
the force of the wind
and the water
to make her laugh
her sinister, little laugh.
Always an adventure
when I ran with her,
black-haired, gypsy girl;
then one morning, she
was gone with the wind.

Running scared

Addicted to adrenaline,
along with the testosterone
swirling in the hot, dry air,
ready to test my bravery.
The men dressed in white
with red handkerchiefs
around their necks and waist,
waiting for the bulls to
be released to run through
the streets of Pamplona,
following in the footsteps
of the ghost of Hemingway.
I feel my heart
pounding, when suddenly
the bulls come charging
down the cobble-stone,
narrow, ancient streets.
I hear the thundering
clap of their hoofs
echoing in my ears.
The men push those
who are slower than them
out of the way,
some fall hard to the ground
rolling to the side to safety,
others run over by the bulls.
The man next to me
is a step slower and
gets gored in the thigh,
His blood spatters
all over my white shirt.
I clearly smell
the bull's foul breath,
feels his spit on my face.
Once the bulls rush by me,
I stop to catch my breath,
scared to death, feeling
more alive than ever before.

Incorrigible Kids

It's a Mother's nature
to be kind, but
mother is mad,
madder than we have
ever seen her,
raging mad
for we, her children,
have been bad,
taking her kindness
for weakness.
We have walked
all over her,
taking her for granted,
making a mess
and not cleaning up
after ourselves;
not attending
to our chores or
caring for her house;
forever fighting,
hurting each other,
as a torrent of tears
fall from her eyes,
her heart is trembling.
Gone her sunny way
of smiling down on us,
now she's spitting fire
to shake us up,
get us to listen,
get us back in line for
refusing to pick up
our toys spewed
all over the yard,
she's taken them away,
to teach us a lesson,
for Mother is mad,
Mother is sad,
for we have been bad.

Waiting on...

Alone in the dark room,
working in the old ways
of photography,
wondering if I caught
that second in time.

Slowly pulling the film
from the rear of the camera.
Being a *chemist,* an *alchemist,*
cooking up the magic,
holding the dripping negative
up to the light,
adding the contact sheet
in anticipation,
apprehension.

I hold my breath
to see the first print,
my first impression.
Did I get what I saw?
Did my subject reveal itself?
Was I quick enough to catch
the fleeting truth of the moment?

        ...the last leaf from
the tall maple tree to fall
upon the unsuspecting back
of the healthy, feeding fawn
or did she startle at that second,
taking off with a start
darting deep into the forest,
as the first snow flurries
of the Winter season
cascade gently down...

In the Crosshairs

In near darkness
each step brings fear
as he stops before
the hen house
starving
for the forest has
been torn down
built upon
the land developed
leaving little room
to roam
to call home
with little kits
waiting in the den
chances must be taken,
slyness forsaken

but suddenly
his sixth sense
overrides all
for he knows
that man is at hand
and the end is near
if he stays here

he bolts for cover
beneath hedges,
darting
into the darkness.

Sitting atop of a huge boulder

The chilling spray washes
over me, leaving me misty eyed
as I watch the gushing water
thunder down the ravine,
down the side of this mountain,
moving with a purpose;
like us, not knowing
where the journey will take it –
collectively each molecule
moves as one
to create positive energy
over the massive boulders,
around them if need be,
nothing can stop its progress,
moving forward with purpose,
even not knowing
what is around the next bend
or down the next freefall;
to come crashing down
into the womb again
of Mother Earth,
she who gives life
to all the molecules there are,
that ever existed.
The sound of the water's
thunder sweet music
to my dancing heartbeat;
the smell of crashing water
fills the air with extra oxygen
forcing my lungs to expand
to gather in all its goodness;
I feel I could levitate
from the world of man;
as the touch of the spray
cleanses my skin and
deep within me,
freeing my thoughts to be
deep in the heart of creation.

Of Proud Blood

The two-legged takers riding
high on his kind
chase after him relentlessly
until finally he finds himself
trapped at the end
of this unknown canyon
with no way to escape
he runs recklessly at them

their rough ropes wrapped
around his bungling neck
pulled tighter and tighter
making breathing impossible
he struggles to free himself
from their restraints
only to be pulled down
trapped finally in the end

with head bowed down
this proud black, muscular
Mustang stallion
with a bold white star
high on his forehead
is dragged along
against his majestic will
fighting with every step

he thinks back to before their
appearance on the open plains,
when he and his kind
ran as one with the wind
as the thunder of their hooves
against the good earth
made him run faster
leading his kind on

only to stop to drink
of the pure, clear water
from the free-flowing river
at the base of the mountain
or to eat the wild green grasses
there in the lush valley
and once watered and fed
to sleep under the star-filled sky

now as they let him drink
from the cool, calm river,
he rears up angrily
with hatred in his heart
breaking free
racing to higher ground
with them following
on those of his kind

he climbs higher and higher
up the slopes of the mountain
never looking back
only up ahead
until there's nowhere to run
at the edge of the world
he takes flight
flying as one with the wind...

Gypsy Fever

You and I follow the
way of the ever-winding
country dirt road
to where fandango music
wakes up the darkness
for the full moon
leads us through
the forgotten forest
into an open field
where a blazing fire
silhouettes fiddlers
stomping their feet
their bows racing
creating magic
time to shine
seizing the moment as
the flamenco dancers,
daringly dressed
in clashing colors,
kick up the dirt,
digging their heels
into the good Earth
whirling around
long into that night,
their laughter loud,
loving life to its fullest,
free under the full moon.

With first light,
we make our way back
down that winding road,
you whirling around,
your raven black hair
whirling wildly around
with the arrival of
of the rising sun;
you laughing loudly
loving life, with
me loving you...

Towering together

Late in the afternoon
we come upon
this ancient ruin
nestled deep
in the dark jungle.
You pull me through
the massive open gates,
covered in thick vines,
you won't wait
to enter the old city
as monkeys squawk
down at us, you look up
to the top of the tower,
high in the sky, then begin
to climb those steep steps,
covered in green moss.
We grow out of breath
as we go on hand
in hand, step for step
into the semi-darkness
to touch the stars
together in the light
of the full moon
we make our way
up to the tower.
Finally falling asleep
arm in arm
to wake to thunder
booming across
the graying dawn
of a new day,
warming the chill
out of the air
in this strange room
long forgotten by time
as your sweet scent
perfumes
the sultry, still air.

Waiting for the rains

The burden of being
a wildebeest,
food for the many
to feast on;
picked off,
pounced upon,
pulled apart,
left for the vultures
and the hyenas
to pick clean,
without a turn
of the head
of those of the herd,
which moves on
without a thought
of their dead brethren.
Thousands of years
traveling the same
trodden worn path
following the rains
bringing new grass
for them to graze on;
thousands of thundering
wildebeests trudging
across the Serengeti,
timeless in appearance,
like clockwork,
always there to feed
the waiting carnivores,
but now the rains
don't come, drought
due to climate change,
their numbers dwindle
disturbing the natural
order of life
on the grasslands.

Snow storm soon

I walk through the woods
alone with my thoughts;
the brisk breeze
sounding like violins
as it passes through
the few leaves
on the many
different types of trees,
oaks, maples, birch that
line this winding path.
A sudden, cymbal-like
clap from over the far
away majestic mountains
wakes me
from my revelry,
brings me back to reality,
but the sweet sway
of the dancing branches,
sounding like oboes,
opens a doorway
for me to escape into,
an unknown world,
so natural, so unlike
the day to day existence
we live in
with its harsh sounds
of people rushing
around to get their day
over and done with, but
here among these trees,
I hum along
to the 8-count concerto,
free to waltz
my way through
this beautiful, Winter day,
far away from
the dissonance sounds
of man's discontent.

Crane's Neck Cove, Long Island

Walking due east at the far end
of West Meadow Beach,
where bathers and beachcombers
enjoy this sun-soaked afternoon,
I venture off, as I have done often,
where the earth emerges into sky-
high cliffs, towering overhead,
the further east you go.
These cliffs create their own kind
of swirling silence to get lost in,
leaving the world behind, walking
along these million-year-old walls,
that record time in the different
layers of rocks; ash gray, copper,
rust red, and chalky white.
The slippery, shiny, black stones,
polished by the lapping waves,
make walking a game of balance.
Soon the sound of laughter isn't
heard, just the seagulls protesting
my being this far from the others.
They love the wild wind these cliffs
create for them to play in; swirling,
whirling, diving and pulling up, so
soon they forget me, as I walk on,
walking back in time with each
step taken, sea salt filling my lungs.
Once sea shells could be found here,
unbroken, beautiful shells, but, now,
just broken pieces line the shoreline.
From out of the cliff's shadows,
a group of male Natives appear,
scantily dressed in deer skin,
carrying fishing nests and tools
to gather up clams and oysters
to feed their families and to trade.
A large cloud covers the sun and
I am brought quickly back to now.

Reading of a Hero's journey

Rich watches, with his three boys,
the chimps chasing after each other,
when suddenly a smaller chimp
is forced off a cliff, landing
into the murky, stagnant water;
the chimp starts to struggle,
wildly flapping his arms,
trying to keep himself afloat
in the six foot deep moat.
The crowd gets frantic watching
the chimp bobbing under.
People are screaming to the staff
to do something to save the chimp.
They stand looking down,
unable or unwilling to help.
Rich's three boys look up to him
with their sky-blue eyes searching
for a solution to what is unfolding
before their very young minds.
Rich finds himself scaling the wall,
diving into the dark, muddy water;
he swims to the chimp, wraps his
arms around the chimp's shoulders.
People are screaming, cheering,
as he pulls the chimp onto the shore.
He can only hear his boys calling him,
"Daddy, Daddy, please save the chimp."
He looks at the limp, still chimp;
tears start to well up in his eyes, when,
then, the chimp's eyes pop open, blink.
Out of the corner of Rich's right eye,
he sees a large, male chimp charging,
He dives into the water, up and over
the wall, into the arms of his wife.
When he looks back the smaller chimp
is finally finding its footing, the other
chimp wildly waving its arms at Rich,
his boys hugging him like never before.

Time-bomb

Exponentially speaking
we are in serious trouble;
there are just too, too many
of us in each other's faces,
and with no place to run
we are colliding like atoms
with each passing day
we grow and grow more
out of control, agitated,
especially knowing
that there is only just
so much land
and we seem to be
getting too crowded
for our own good, for
the good of human kind;
from the icy tundra
to the tropical rain forests
to the driest of deserts,
we are everywhere,
we can't afford to get
on each other's nerves,
not enough room for that,
and there is no more living
large in our arrogance
for now we live with wars
over clean water,
people fighting for food,
our environment injured
by us careless children,
conflicts between the haves
and have-nots on the horizon,
as more and more of us
continue to appear
from out of nowhere,
we sit on our hands
hoping hard, praying,
that we can outlast
the tinderbox of time, but
the clock is ticking, ticking…   25

A Spring day in the desert

You awake wanting to do
something hot,
where your sweat
is pulled from your body,
cooling you off;
you want to dance in
the towering shadow of
the Saguaro Cactus
standing strong against
the silhouette
of the dawning of day;
to trek down a road-less,
backcountry wilderness,
hats, sunscreen, water
ready for the sizzling sun
to go where roadrunners
chase lazy lizards
from their sunbathing
off of orange-tan rocks.
You want to witness
hovering hummingbirds
fly above, kissing
the bright violet flowers
of a hedgehog cactus.
You want to run
your long fingers over
the drawn Petroglyphs
on massive boulders,
telling of a time
when Natives ran wild
over this land;
to hear, to feel,
the screech owl's hoot
as dusk descends.
You want to bask
in the orange/blue/violet
stunning setting sun,
then go home to dream.

A Father's Wish

Our first-time stargazing,
on this cold, cloudless,
January night arrayed
with a million stars,
you pick one

to point out to me,
asking how far
away this light
comes to us
from out of the dark?

Wondering
how it would be
to travel out
among the stars
soaring there

to that guiding light
on this clear night
searching the heavens.
I think:
that bright light

may have faded
long ago
and is now
only a remnant
of what once was...

looking to the stars,
closing my eyes,
I squeeze your hand,
whispering a wish
across time and space.

They watch in horror

Mother and daughter
are playing in the backyard
with Angel and
their new puppy, Coco.
The tiny, Yorkie-Tzu dog
runs around and around,
refusing to be caught,
no matter how hard
they try to grab her.
They both are laughing
at Coco's antics,
the more they try to catch
her the faster she runs.
They think they've got her
cornered, but she bolts
past them into an open area.
Suddenly from out of nowhere
a red-tailed hawk descends
down upon them.
The hawk digs its talons
into the small back of Coco,
lifting the dog up into the sky.
They can hear Coco crying,
they start screaming.
Valerie picks up some stones,
starts flinging them
at the escaping thief.
Her Mother falls to her knees,
crying her heart out,
she can't watch anymore,
but Valerie watches Coco
wiggling, snapping at
the legs of the hawk.
Then suddenly the hawk
let's go of Coco, who falls
20 feet to the ground,
bouncing up, barking at
the disappearing hawk.

New to the neighborhood

Out our back door on
our low concrete brick wall
a large, male Raven
eating the innards
of some scavenged steal;
holding it down with a claw,
pulling, tearing at it
with that powerful beak;
throwing back his head
swallowing it whole.
Seeing Coco and I,
he takes two quick steps
towards us, pushing
out his iridescent chest.
"Hello, Blackie," I call.
He fluffs out his head feathers,
making him appear larger.
"Sorry to interrupt your meal."
Coco begins to bark wildly
at this dark stranger.
Who with a hop, hop, hop,
a caw, caw, caw,
Blackie flies up into the air
landing high on our roof,
staring, glaring at Coco.
Caw, caw, caw, with
Coco still barking, until
Blackie swoops down,
spreading his wings, casting
a large shadow over Coco,
who quickly becomes quiet,
hiding behind me.
Blackie back at his prize,
we watch in awe
as he eats until full,
then with a hop, hop, hop
he flies away to wherever
Ravens go off to…

"Free at last, free at last"

From my beach chair seat,
I watch my five-year-old
daughter, Valerie,
pick up a bucket, then
empty it into the green sea.
I watch a group of children
rush up to the bucket,
emptying the contents
from the small fishing net.
I watch my daughter
wait until they wildly run
back down to the shoreline.
She takes the bucket and
empties it again; then
there appears on the horizon
the group of six
descending down upon
my daring daughter.
I watch with amazement
as she takes off running,
the kids chase after her.
In hot pursuit, I catch up
as they surround her
like a swarm of flies.
I pick her up
in the middle
of the shouting mob,
fists raised in the air.
"Who do you think you are
letting go of our fish?"
We walk away from them,
hand in hand,
she looks up to me, "Daddy,
I had to free those minnows.
We are all God's creatures."

Honored

While on my late morning walk,
I hear a familiar "caw, caw, caw"
high overhead, Blackie the Raven,
my early morning friend who I get
to see while having my green tea,
and sneaking him a dog treat as
we cordially speak to one another.
I watch him fly in wide circles
around and around slowly
making his way down
to hop, hop, hop atop
the low concrete brick wall
to finally come to a stop
just six feet away
from where I am standing.
I sit as near as my fear will allow.
His black, beady eyes
lock onto, into mine,
staring, while twisting his head.
I can feel them searching deep,
seeking to know my soul,
for he knows the neighbors throw
stones at him when within range.
Making wa-wa-warbling noises,
reeling his head and back forth,
fluffing out his head feathers,
he talks, I listen intently
for at least ten minutes,
watching the world pass us by
before some passing truck
blasts out its ugly horn,
sending Blackie to hop, hop, hop,
caw, caw, caw, and, then,
with two strong swoops
of his wings brings him
high above the trees tops,
airborne with the swift breeze,
off to wherever he goes…

Stardust child

My dear, dear daughter,
so daring and darling
as you dance the shoreline,
playing tag with the frigid
incoming tide, making sure not
to let it touch your bare feet
for you know how cold
it is this March morning.

Dancing with stardust sparkling
in your sky blue eyes,
kicking up the wet sand,
glad that Spring is finally
about to sing your favorite song
of warmth and wonder after
a long, hard Winter.
Oh, how you have waited!

Fascinated by flight
you run through a flock of seagulls
to watch them take off,
flapping your arms as if wings;
lost in laughter
after they are airborne.
You wave them goodbye for now,
wishing you could join them.

I look to the heavens,
sending out a kiss,
to thank my lucky stars for you
are the dream of your
Mother's and my love;
that could only come from above
with your lust of life,
so full of stardust…

Dreams of wings

Watching from the safety
of being deep
in the center of the circle
of a thousand chicks
running up and down
the crowded shoreline,
she watches her parents and
many other adult flamingos
take a running start
facing into the strong wind
to take off in flight
with their long necks
stretched out and their
long legs trailing behind
they look like fire flames
streaking across the sky,
flapping their wings riding
high on the wind currents,
their perfect reddish-pink
feathers glistening
on the sun rays
of the dawning new day
as they fly in formation.
In awe of them,
she practices every day,
while one of her parents
watches over her.
Her puffy, gray down
hasn't spouted out
the feathers needed
to get up off the ground,
but each day she runs
faster along the sandy shore,
practicing running while
flapping her tiny wings.
Exhausted, she rests
in her mud-mound nest,
dreaming of being airborne…

Where da rabbit?

Our walks aren't the same
ever since Coco,
our 5lb. Yorkie-Tzu,
first saw that rabbit
hiding in the bushes,
suddenly darting out,
catching Coco off guard,
but somewhere in her
genetic make-up
she knew her job
was to catch and shake
it to smithereens.
Now each walk is like
a military mission
to track down the enemy,
to go behind the lines
to find where it hides.
Pulling me feverishly
with sheer determination
from the minute we
step outside our door,
her black nose is
pounding the ground,
up and down she goes,
around and around
every bush,
sniffing every inch,
until finally she flushes
out a big jack rabbit,
far bigger than her,
the rabbit bolts with
Coco in quick pursuit,
choking at the end of
the length of her leash,
dead in her tracks,
growling like a grizzly,
up on her hind legs as
the rabbit hightails away.

Spill, baby, spill

We've grown too slick
for something like this
to ever happen to us,
or so we thought;
but the gushing crude
from the bottom
of the vast ocean
wildly rushes
up and out
into the warm water;
the shifting winds
pushes the waves
to speed, spread the oil
toward the shoreline,
a race we are losing
as the oil washes ashore,
toward the wildlife refuges,
where it's breeding season
for all the species
of shorebirds
along the southern shore
of the Gulf Coast;
the little chicks arriving
upon our earth
into this unfolding horror
and their parents,
are sitting ducks,
covered in oil
unable to fly away;
as our little game
of Russian roulette
we willingly play
with our environment
for our lust of fossil fuel
has the gun going off,
shooting down dead
these birds without
them ever having
a chance to take flight.

Gulping us up

The old fisherman,
with rough, ruddy cheeks,
deep lines in his face
from laughing, telling
countless fish stories,
gulps back the tears.
Robert Summers,
5th generation shrimper,
been fishing the delta
since boyhood,
just now recovering
from cruel Katrina,
but this man-made mess,
a morphing mass
of oil forming a slick
that is drifting up the coast
to the marshes and wetlands
has him landlocked
a lot longer than he likes.
Wearing a grimace,
so stern it's sad for his boat
been docked for weeks.
He can't take her out,
not in that slick.
"Get all gulped up."
His hands hold tight
to the wooden helm
of his beloved boat,
staring out at the spill,
spreading wider across
the morning horizon.
"Water once was clear,
clear to the bottom,
now just darkness."

He looks to his grandson,
standing by his side,
wraps his arm around
the boy's shoulder,
then begins to cry.

Wishing I could run with them

Miles away from where I stand, waiting
on this low-lying ridge,
the taste of red clay fills my throat,
making it hard to even swallow,
the swirling, whirling cloud
of red dust and dirt storms
across the floor of the canyon,
a dried out, ancient river bed lost to time.

What spooked that first stallion or mare?
What stroked their fear to start
the whole herd to stampede?
A rattlesnake? A gopher's hole?
There's no way to know, but
off and running as one they are,
being pushed tightly together
by the narrowing of the canyon's walls.

It seems mere seconds before they are
upon me, sucking the breath from me
by the sheer, urgent energy
of the swirling, whirling wind within
these massive, majestic, ageless walls,
pulling me into this passing vortex
of hundreds of horses' blurred bodies
rushing by me. I hide behind a boulder.

The sweet scent of their combined sweat
permeates the dry, dusty air being
forced into my nostrils. The howling
of their hooves near deafening
against the hard red clay. Their wildness
vibrates through every cell in my body.
I watch as they disappear around the far
bend at the end of the canyon walls.

The Cleansing

I've come this way
countless times,
but today, for some reason,
maybe it's the way
the wind is swirling,
a new path appears,
well-worn, dug deep
into the good Earth.
Pulled onward, a silence,
a stillness, surrounds me;
feeling eyes on me
with each step I take
deeper into the forest,
ancient eyes, wise eyes
watch as I finally come
to a clearing,
with spiraling trees
shooting high into the sky
creating a cathedral
effect around me;
I whisper, an echo answers.
All the while through
an opening in the leaves,
sunlight spotlights
an old stone altar
with strange symbols
written on both sides.
I feel compelled to kneel,
to touch down to the ground,
and in an instant,
I feel warm all over, blessed,
kissed by the Goddess
of the Wilderness.
I don't remember how
I got home, but I know
I knew not to look back;
wondering of the wanderers
who, too, have graced this place.

Our Rivers within

We stand together,
holding hands,
feeling the mighty mist
of the melting snow
splash across our faces,
making you laugh.
How gentle the spray,
how gentle your laugh,
how alive,
it tingles, tickles
your buoyant spirit...
Eons ago, these two
wild rivers
ran free of the other,
descending down
the steep slopes
of these mountain sides,
racing through valleys
creating canyons,
working their way
towards one another
across time and space
until they collide,
come alive, together;
gushing, rushing, as
if their forces of nature
brought them together
to run as one.
You can hear their love
for one another
whispered on the wind
as they rush by, flowing
out to the distant sea,
to live out their destiny –
like you and I, our forces
of nature brought us
together to live out
our destinies as one.

To provide and protect

Hidden high in the cliff wall
the four Bald Eagle chicks
ravenously chirping, waiting
for their parents to return,
both out to feed their needs.

Hissing while slithering up
the slope of the mountain
a rattlesnake sneaks
between the boulders,
sensing an easy meal.

From high in the sky
Mother eagle comes home
with a struggling mole
grasped tight in her talons,
but upon seeing the rattlesnake

she lets go of the mole,
who bounces twice
on a patch of grass,
then rolls for a short while
before scooting into the bush.

Nosediving down Mother takes
hold of the rattler's tail and
with a steep climb upward she
pulls that snake up into the air
flying far away from their cave.

She drops the snake down onto
the big boulders below; badly
beaten and bruised the snake
slithers away to heal and
hide from the sizzling sun.

Dawning Sun

The lush green of Spring
is succulent in the Summer
with the morning sun
coming over the mountains,
slowly making its way
across the still water
of the large, freshwater lake,
where we go to be alone.
We watch from our porch
in wooden rocking chairs,
with no need to talk,
breathing in pine scent,
as the sun slices through
the man-made path
between the tall pines,
so tall their green
disappears into blue.
We watch it warm the beach,
watch the sand glisten,
watch it spread up the slope
of green grass leading to us.
Suddenly a silver fish
flies out from the still surface
to snap up a large, white moth,
sending lashing ripples across
the water with its splash,
awakening the loons, whose cry
looms large, echoing through
the tall pine trees to our ears,
waking us up with a start
as the sun's light starts
to slowly climb up our
three gray, wooden steps.
Soon the sun will shine upon
your face and you will smile,
loving its warmth, and I
will laugh like I always do.

An early morning sighting

The large, male Mourning dove,
coos, ever-watchful
as his smaller mate
pecks between the pebbles,

foraging for food
for their two squabs
resting, waiting
back at the nest.

They search for the seed
that I throw over the wall
for all the birds
to come feast on each day

Startled by a passing bicycle,
they fly off in opposite
directions, wings rapidly waving
goodbye in the face of danger.

Parting ways, until they loop
around on the breezeless air
this warming Spring morning,
to quickly return

to one another, with
the tips of their wings
appearing to touch,
they fly off together

I reach over to you,
touching your hand,
you smile, as the two lovers
disappear from my view.

Touched by human hands

Taken from out of the wild,
taken in the back of a SUV
this baby bison,
then returned to the herd.

Rejected by the herd,
who run wide of the calf,
circling ever wider away, while
he wildly bleats for his mother.

Confused, lost, alone, forsaken,
the calf dashes off
in any directions
searching, but shunned.

Then rejected by his mother,
who can't sniff her child's scent,
lost is his smell of the wild,
tainted, touched, not to be trusted.

Circling in a swirl of dust
in ever smaller circles, until
finally falling to his knees,
then he rolls over to his side.

Taken from the herd, having been
imprinted on people, not by bison;
suddenly a sharp stab of the needle
into his hindquarters; sleepy, until

finally falling to his knees,
slowly rolling over onto his side,
confused, lost, alone, tainted
by those two legged beasts.

Touched by a human child

Heart wrenching watching
that young boy fall head first
into the gorilla pit,
hitting his skull hard against
the cold, concrete floor.

Witnessing events unfold,
unable to move, frozen in fear
by the strange "splatt" sound
and the tiny cries emanating
from the young child below.

17 year old, Harambe,
a Western Lowland, male gorilla,
came grunting out from his cave
to where the boy laid crying.
Bowing down, he sniffs *"human."*

Grabbing the boy by his ankles,
dragging him back to his cave
with the boy's head banging
as he is pulled along.
He stands guard at the opening.

10 minutes he hid the boy
in the darkness of his cave;
standing, agitated, disoriented
by this turn of events.
'Was he just protecting the boy?'

But to the Zookeepers
the child's life was in danger.
A quick decision had to be made;
the choice was easy –
so they shot the animal dead.

Unable to move, unable to talk,
wondering where the parents were?
Knowing a gorilla's parent would
never have let such a thing happen.   44

A day away from the World

You knew of this secret place, so
like a lovely, little nymph
of the forest, you fly
past the trees of all kinds.
I follow close behind
trying to keep from falling.

Trees so thick you can't
see this hidden swimming hole
deep in the forest with its
crystal clear, pristine water,
blue from the bubbling hot springs
that waits for those in the know.

I stop in wonder to witness
the small waterfall at the far end,
that feeds this mirror-like pool,
since the wind can't get in
to create even a ripple,
I revel in your reflection.

You let go of my hand, running
into the water, laughing and
splashing in the 30-ft. deep hole
as I try to catch you, to hold onto the
dream that you are, but you swim
away, playing with my emotions.

You leave the water to disappear
into the thick of the trees, only to
reappear at the top of a 20-ft. cliff.
Waving as you do a perfect swan dive
creating such a tiny splash as you laugh
coming up for air from your daring dive.

We swim to the far end to hide behind
the waterfall's curtain to kiss as the
warm water rolls over us. I hold you,
wanting to never let go, to live here
with you hidden from the world.   45

On top of the world

Alone
on this Colorado mountain
with perfect, powdery snow,
just above the tree line,
looking down upon the valley below,
watching the ant-like people
zig-zagging around each other;
with air so rare that it has
no taste or smell, so crisp and clear;
when out of the forest walks
a large, tawny, male lynx,
with its long, pointed, tufted ears,
short stubby tail and large paws
that work like snowshoes;
it parades past me,
strolling along the ski slope,
at home on this mountainous terrain.
I am shocked and silent,
standing as still as I can on skis,
for normally nocturnal, rarely seen,
hunting only at night
so I know this is a gift
given to me from the gods
to be so close to something so wild,
so close I see its shiny, bright eyes,
from where it gets its name,
and the white fur on its underside.
It looks my way, stopping
for a second, sniffing the cold air,
but seemingly without
a care in the world that
I am here on the same slope as he.
Wishing I had my cellphone
to snap a photo as proof
of my good fortune, but I left
it down in my room,
so, this great gift is for me
alone.

Today they play

The two polar bear cubs,
with their tiny black eyes
and black noses that
stand out against
their pure white fur
dash out from the den,
Mother bear pokes her head
out to keep an eye on them.
They chase after each other,
biting one another's hindquarters
as they come crashing
through the few pines trees.
One suddenly stops
rears up on his back legs,
pounces upon his sister,
they tumble back
rolling around in the snow,
until the sister starts
to dart away, then, when
he catches up with her they hug,
but soon they are swatting
their paws, pushing,
and shoving each other.
She grabs his short stub of a tail,
which gets a yelp out of him,
he thrashes through three pine trees
to get at her, but the trees become
their new target, they strip bare
the branches of all their needles,
then he seems to remember
and begins biting her back,
now she's on the attack.
Mother bear watches them play,
knowing soon will come the day
when they will leave this den,
knowing each new Spring brings
less ice, making hunting harder.

El Cajon Pass, California

Thinking you and I are off
for a weekend away
in the mountains, alone, but
then, we came to a dead stop.
Seeing people fleeing from
their cars as far as the eye
could see up the winding road.
The season of high risk makes
the dry brush and timber
a great fuel, then
with a wild wind
blowing up the slope
the fire jumps the highway,
engulfing abandoned cars,
bursting into flames
as people try to run to safety.
This fast-moving wind
just needed a spark – now
2,000 acres up in smoke.
Suddenly a tractor-trailer
catches on fire,
it ignites, as a huge,
black, billowing plume
blows due west,
rising above the mountains,
covering like a fog, only
it's the color of darkness.
Finally, finding safety
with the EMTs,
we hug, holding onto
one another tightly.
The smell of burning rubber
burns our eyes and lungs,
making you begin to cry.
"This is just the beginning
of wildfire season and
with this drought who knows
the hell we are going to see."

Letting go slowly

My wandering has lead me here
where this rivulet steps down
the side of the cliff's face,
5 – 1 ft. steps, black, slick slate

I sit on the third step letting
the cold, streaming, refreshing water
roll over me, fast and furious,
feeling the flowing pressure

on every muscle group, moving
to a new muscle every few minutes,
taking my time, taking it all in,
feeling them let go, ease up

finally, fully relaxed like never before,
each muscle aligning themselves,
becoming part of my whole being
deep, deep, down to the core of my soul

freeing my thoughts to flow
like never before, connected,
I see, hear, feel, taste and smell
the world around me like never before

the cold of the water warmed by
the tingling of my synapses as
their pulses race throughout my body,
electrifying, revitalizing, rejuvenating

deep, deep, down to my molecular level
I see, hear, feel, taste, smell, know
that I have never let go like this before;
the water is having its way with me

as if this water is kissing me,
impossible to resist, like only a lover
would do every inch of my being
being loved all at once, kissed within…

49

Having the wind within

We wander across the dark maroon,
rocky waterfront with a wind
so stern we are completely alone,
except for dozens of seagulls riding
on the waves of the wind.

You wearing your yellow sun hat,
tied tight, with its wide brim
shading your already rosy cheeks
from the strong, Autumn sun
of this Indian Summer day.

The sea stormy, the crashing waves
playing a symphony, and a blue as
beautiful as your crystal, clear eyes,
so clear one can see into
the innocence of your soul,

as we walk without words,
holding hands when the rocks
get too daunting; you smiling
every time you get back to
a solid footing to walk ahead

for this wind doesn't upset you,
no, instead it seems to inspire
your spirit to dance across
where the wet, hard-packed
sand is found between the rocks.

Seagulls swoop down to hear
your siren voice sing out songs
long ago forgotten that come
to you with every breath of
this wild wind that you take in.

You lovingly laugh when
nearly free from gravity to
finally come back down
to Earth, to kiss again and again...   50

The busy Bee Keeper

Valerie slowly moves her way,
making sure not to
make any waves,
over to the still bee,
exhausted from fighting
for its freedom, trapped on
the surface of the pool water.
She comes up from behind,
cupping the bee in her hands,
scooping it up and out of
the pool to safety.
"Be careful," I scold.
"You could get stung!"
Not listening,
she watches intently
for any movement,
for any sign of life,
standing shoulder high
in the cool, blue water.
"I've watched you do it.
I do it just like you, Daddy."
Suddenly the bee gets busy,
buzzing those wings
rapidly, coming back to life,
then it lifts itself off the tiles,
circles around and around
for a few times, then flies
away off into the blue skies.
"There are too few bees
these days, Daddy.
Fewer and fewer each year,
and they are so dear to me.
Didn't you tell me,
"They kiss the flowers,
which brings us our honey?"
She crosses her arms
under the water and gives
me a firm nod with her head.

A date with my daughter

Valerie saw the commercial
for the Ocean Conservatory,
read their website; learned
how to be a team member;
learned that our oceans
provide us the air we breathe,
the food we need to eat,
and the water we drink.
She knows it to be
the home of dolphins,
whales, seals, and
so many of the animals
that she loves so dearly,
so she set in motion
for us to be volunteers
after learning how the oceans
are dying due to man
throwing his trash,
waste from power plants
straight into the seas.
On our next vacation
we walk the shoreline
of our favorite beach
in sunny West Coast Florida,
collecting plastics bottles,
aluminum cans, recyclables
left behind by beachgoers.
I hold the biodegradable bags
as she deposits the debris in
to be picked up later.
We weren't alone,
many families join in
having fun together
under the scorching sun.
We walk and talk,
watching dolphins suddenly
appear on the horizon.
"I think they are thanking us."

Rainforest of the Sea

When first married
we honeymooned off
the coast of Southern Florida,
snorkeling in its warm waters
around wondrous coral reefs;
amazed by their diversity,
amazed by the colors,
amazed by how teeming full
of plants and fish
living symbiotically
providing food and shelter
for one another
in their underwater forest.
Amazed by how they formed,
a living colony of tiny coral,
each secreting a chemical,
calcium carbonate,
a form of limestone,
building upon itself
over countless years.
30 years later, we revisit
these warm waters
only to witness
a visible decline,
a "bleaching" has begun-
the delicate balance
of growth and erosion
has been upset-
we could see it everywhere
in these now warmer waters.
Amazed by how alarming
the change is in our lifetime
we worry, ruining
our second honeymoon,
will our grandchildren get
to grace this special place or
will this too begin to disappear
like the rainforests everywhere?

Sea of Tranquility

While my wife and daughter
search the long shoreline
for perfect seashells:
the warm water
of the Gulf of Mexico
rolls calmly over me,
so salty I float
like a happy manatee
free with each ripple
of the next wave
washing gently over me,
caressing me,
allowing all my worries
to sink to the sandy bottom,
as the sun showers
down its strong rays,
bringing a glow to my face,
I stare up to the heavens,
with my sunglasses on,
wandering aimlessly,
without wondering
about work,
wars unjustly waged;
I just float along
allowing the waves
to have their way with me,
take me where they will
I go freely, growing more
and more relaxed
like a fetus inside
its Mother's womb
gently being rocked
without a care in the world,
with my arms by my side
I bob up and down,
all is forgotten
and forgiven
as I just float happily along,
staring up to the heavens.

Blood Ivory

Believers see their lord
when they look upon
Christ on the cross

carved from the tusks
of the ivory
poached from the elephants.

Those whose lives
are ruled by superstition
wear ivory amulets

around their necks
to protect them from harm
of black magic.

Neither see the killing fields
of the countless elephants'
carcasses left to rot in the hot sun.

Maybe, if they were near to hear
the fear in the anguished
last breaths before death,

for these elephants know from
their ancestor's remains
what is going to happen,

maybe then, and, only then
will human kind step in to stop
this senseless slaughter.

Time to breathe, again

They have always been here
from the dawning
of our awareness,
always been there for the taking.
Gifts given to be used
over and over
renewed with each new day.
No need to dig,
no need to drill,
no need to scar Mother Earth,
no need to cut her to her core.
They have always been here,
the rush of the wind,
the thrust of flowing water,
the smiling sun warming us,
like a loving Mother.
No need to dig,
no need to drill,
no need for Mother's black
blood to seep
from deep within her soul;
blackening our world,
destroying our precious air
we need to breathe, while
making a gaping hole
in our atmosphere,
letting our inside out.
They have always been here;
we need to use them, not abuse
these gifts given.
So there is no need to dig,
no need to drill;
the more we do
the sooner we will kill
our garden of Eden.
Is this the gift we want
to leave our children,
a living hell on earth?

Over-population

The deer, a whole boat load,
were brought here
to this uninhabited island
off the coastline of Alaska
to feed the miners.
The miners had been told
there was gold to be had,
but it was a bust,
only fool's gold.
They bore deep only to find
iron-ore at the core
of this tiny island.
The herd of deer
set free when the last men
leave the island;
also left behind,
scars from their digging
and dynamiting
of the once lush hillsides,
now time to heal, again,
now that man is gone.
Except for a few harmless birds
that stopped-over on migration,
there were no predators
to cull the deer population,
so they grew and grew and
as their numbers exponentially
grew out of control
soon all the greenery was eaten,
then all the lichen was eaten up,
then the herd begins to thin,
first the elderly and sick,
soon the fawns are gone,
then extinction of their species
on this tiny island. Again,
the island is uninhabited,
except for a few flocks of birds
just passing through.

57

Whispers on the wind

The Elders of the village,
gray-bearded, bent over,
by time and the great weight
of all their wisdom, come out
of the forest, out of the mist
of the early morning, with
the sun rising, we follow,
follow in their footsteps,
out of the forest
down through the valley
to where the Six Trees
stand alone, stand together
from the time of our first fire
the Elders have met here
on the edge of the cliff
overlooking our lake.
The Elders observe
the dead fish that line the shore,
no animals drink or gather here,
the water black, still, lifeless;
more and more often
the ground shakes, rumbles;
the snows grow less and less
each year, so less river water.
The Elders gather together
under the canopy of the trees,
among the great roots that
intertwine these six massive oaks,
they sit and talk for hours, talk
of the sun-scorching summers
turning soil to dust,
they can taste it in the air,
something is astir,
they've heard the words
of fear from the forest
being whispered on the wind:
it's time to climb the hills,
up into the mountains,
where our ancestors have gone
before in times of great unrest.

A Place in the Sun

The tall, old oak trees
tower over all others,
without a care for
the rest in the forest,
they touch the sky,
while all others
try hard to reach out
over each other,
fighting, pushing
to any opening,
making the most
of any opportunity,
branching out,
sprouting up
wherever a glimmer
of the sun's warm rays
shine through.
Those old oaks on top
move in unison,
filling the voids,
soaking in the sun's
golden glory,
without a care
or concern
for those under them,
as their roots grow,
reaching out,
robbing as much
water as possible
to ensure success,
they work both ends,
at the great cost
to those around them,
blocking the view,
stopping all progress
if it means sharing
their source of strength:
no sense in doing that...

An albatross around our necks

He forced me, against
my will to come witness
our garbage traveling
far across the ocean,
floating on the current
to the tiny atoll of Midway,
dead in the middle
of the Pacific Ocean.
Our throw-away culture,
where everything
is disposable,
impacting the inhabitants,
killing many thousands
of albatross chicks
after they eat chunks
of our plastics that
they mistake for food
that we just toss
away without a worry
of where it might end up,
tossed away after
being used only once;
bearing witness firsthand
those baby birds
flapping around,
gagging as they choke
to finally flop down dead
on the sandy beach
to quickly decompose
due to the heat,
the rain, and the insects,
thousands of dead birds
litter the beautiful beach,
their decomposed feathers
and the eaten plastics
are all that remains...

Dreaming of being airborne

In early Spring, off the desert,
the zoom of the wind
rushes, brushes, past my face,
puts me in the zone as I walk
alone along a busy highway,
not twenty feet away;
but I look to the east for solace,
endless desert of the Reservation
runs into the base
of far off mountain ranges
extending deep into Mexico.
The breeze exhilarating as
it ripples the hairs on my arms,
the whoosh of that wind
sending a shiver up my spine
as I walk within
the tunnel the trees make
flight seem not just a dream,
thrusting my arms up and out
like they were wings, with
the wind singing of its freedom,
ringing in my ears, soaring,
roaring deep down
into, onto, my brain waves,
beating its way around
down to my wild heart,
lifting-up my spirit, up off
of this good Earth, a rebirth;
knowing going home
with the wind at my back
how easy it will be to dream
of taking flight, gliding off
at the highest point
of this walk, up-drafting,
riding the thermals
higher and higher;
like a bold, bald eagle flying
above it all, one with the wind…

This little game she likes to play

Our walks in the woods are always
an adventure when Coco,
our 5 1/2 lbs. Yorkie-Tzu comes along,
always at the end of her leash
leading the way down this worn path
we have made over her four years with us.
She sniffs the air, her nemesis is near,
a young, female, coyote kit
who seems to love to annoy little Coco
with her tiny yips from the shadows
in the bushes just ahead of us.
Coco yapping and choking herself,
going completely, uncontrollably loco.
I have to laugh being dragged along
after the teasing coyote kit,
loving being in on this little game.
I see flashes of the kit dart in front of us
from bush to bush until Coco is exhausted,
then she disappears back into the forest.

But today with Spring beginning to sing
it's song of warmth again, that crazy kit
has come to taunt little Coco
on her own territory, her own turf.
Coco can't contain herself for there
in our front yard, there on our grass,
playing with Coco's favorite toy, she is
tossing it high in the air, then
chasing wildly after the toy,
yipping as if laughing,
only now four times bigger than Coco.
She stops to stare Coco down,
while Coco is yapping and scratching
away on the screen door.
I fear she will tear through the screen
and close the door. Coco runs around
and around the room non-stop,
as the kit disappears back into the forest.

Learning to laugh loudly

With no wind and a strong sun,
we come out of the sweet, pine-
scented forest into a clearing
where you pull on my hand,
stopping me in my stride.
With a finger over your lips,
you point at two black spots
rolling down the slight slope
about 50 feet ahead of us;
two ravens coming to a stop.
Shaking off the snow,
they rear their black heads
back and forth, fluffing
out their shiny feathers,
looking like they were laughing,
making loud cooing noises
as they side-step their way up
to have another and another run
down that snow-covered hill.
We watch in wonder,
huddled together to keep warm,
making sure not to move, while
they play for quite a few runs.
When enough fun for one day,
they make click-clocking noises,
bouncing up together twice,
soon to be over the far hills,
we watch until they disappear.

Like little children we run, hand
in hand up that slope to roll down,
laughing loudly when we finally
come to a full stop at the bottom
of this snow-covered valley.
We shake off all the snow
and go up for another run,
wondering the whole while
where those ravens were off to…

Your Cancerian soul

We wander the woods together
going deeper into the forest,
until we hear a shot ring out
shattering the sweet silence

You seem pulled to the sound
of where we heard a heavy thump.
There lays a doe shot
through the heart, stone dead.

I watch as you know to go
closer to the dead deer,
there lies her fawn, so close
to her mother's warm belly.

I see a tear well up in your eyes
as you pick up the fawn,
who lets you as you speak slowly
soft, soothing words to her.

I see your motherhood embrace
this now motherless child.
I see her wildness let go
as if she knows to trust you.

I watch you wrap her up warm
in one of your own blankets.
I watch you give her water
from your long, loving fingertips.

I see a tear well up in your eyes
as you hand her over, with one last
sniff of her innocence, this blessing,
to the wild refuge worker.

I watch you cry in the car,
falling in love with you once, again.

A Life Well Lived

The crushing, crackling
rush of my heavy boots
crashing through the frozen
top inch of newly fallen snow,
the first of this Winter season,
is the music I march to
to keep me warm down
this off-the-trail path
that I notched out
eons ago when I was a boy,
each tree taking me deeper
into this forest, with the way
marked for my return back.
I've grown to know
the sweet scent of each tree,
grown to know them
as living, breathing beings,
growing with me each year
I'm lucky to pass their way.
I come upon an old friend,
I knew him as Carl.
His fresh coyote carcass
gaunt, most of his teeth gone,
slowly warming its way
deeper into the snow.
I got a sad, sinking feeling.
I've seen Carl, Sally,
his smaller mate,
and their many cute kits
cross my path priceless times.
Often seen Carl with a rabbit
clenched between his canines.
Flurries begin to cover Carl.
In the Spring, again, I will
wander this forest alone, but
I've never been alone here.
I'll stop along the way
to pay my respects to him.

"Lonesome George" died today

June 24th, 2012,
it is a sad day today,
George was the last
of his subspecies,
Chelonidis nigra abingdoni.
He was the last of
the Pinta Island Tortoises,
symbol of the Galapagos,
found stretched out
near his watering hole,
over 100 years old,
out-living all those
of his kind.
He had roamed the island
of Santa Cruz in the Galapagos
searching to find
another to breed with.
I wonder if he remembered
in the last firing of his synapses
of the slaughter done
by whalers and fishermen,
nearly bringing his kind
to extinction in the early days?
And, then, when the wild goats
were introduced to the island,
they soon exponentially
grew out of control,
decimating the vegetation,
slowing, painfully
killing his kind
when there wasn't enough to eat.
I wonder if he knew
he was the last to roam this earth?
I wonder how the last
human will feel when they roam
this earth alone?

Under the Weather Requiem

If you care
   to listen,
hear the wicked wind twisting,
whipping, ripping, stripping away
all that lays in its path,
its angry howling
like hungry wolves,
hear Mother's cry…

If you care
   to listen,
hear the rain beating down hard
and heavy, carrying away all
that isn't anchored to the earth,
its screaming
like an abusive man,
hear Mother's plea…

If you care
   to listen,
hear the cracking of the dry
dirt due to drought
being pulled, torn apart
like an open wound,
no more tears to shed,
hear Mother's pain…

If you care
   to listen,
hear the searing of the burning
trees, sizzling of their leaves
as it spreads across
like a high fever
stealing the life of a child,
hear Mother's anguish…

If you care
        to listen,
hear Mother's heart breaking,
sighing in surrender,
being pulled asunder,
assaulted from all sides,
caused by those children of hers
who never cared to listen…

First they came for…*in honor of Martin Niemoller*

First they came for the elephants,
came for their ivory, left their carcasses
to rot under the mean sun,
and I did not speak out
because I was not an elephant.

Then they destroyed the homeland
of the polar bears, without a care
as it melted away into a wasteland,
and I did not speak out
because I was not a polar bear.

Then they poisoned the drinking water
of the inner cities to save money,
wasting away the minds of the young ones,
and I did not speak out
because I could afford bottled water.

Then they polluted our air
so the young, the elderly, the sick
couldn't breathe, slowly suffering,
and I did not speak out
because I still lived my life as they died.

When in cold-blood they killed our Earth,
suddenly there is no place for me to live,
so we few left alive huddle together
to cry out at ourselves for not stopping the
ticking of our own home-made time-bomb…